The Economic Performance of the ASEAN Economies from the Mid-1990s

Anne Booth

Professor of Economics (With Reference to Asia)
SOAS, University of London

April 2009

About the Author

Anne Booth is Professor of Economics (With Reference to Asia) at the School of Oriental and African Studies, University of London. She has published extensively on contemporary and historical development in South East Asia. Recent major publications include: *Colonial Legacies: Economic Development in East and South East Asia* (University of Hawaii Press 2007).

The Economic Performance of the ASEAN Economies from the Mid-1990s

The ASEAN Economies After the Crisis: What Are the Issues?

From the 1960s to the 1990s several economies in Southeast Asia (Singapore, Malaysia, Thailand and Indonesia) achieved rapid and sustained economic growth rates, and considerable improvements in the living standards of their populations.[1] It was these growth rates which led the World Bank to characterise these economies, (along with Japan, Hong Kong, South Korea and Taiwan) as 'Asian Miracles', whose economic performance had, according to the World Bank, important lessons for other parts of the developing world.[2] The 1993 World Bank report was cautious about treating China as a miracle economy (it was written in the immediate aftermath of the Tiananmen Square uprising) although it did acknowledge that the creation of the special economic zones in the south of the country was leading to rapid growth of exports in that region. Countries such as India and Vietnam were given scant attention, except as negative examples of 'inward-looking' economies whose policies were not likely to support rapid growth in the immediate future.

How much difference a decade makes. To many observers of the contemporary Asian economic scene, the legacy of the 'Asian crisis' seems fairly clear. The major economies of Southeast Asia, and especially those most severely affected by the crisis (Thailand and Indonesia) have been slow to recover from the aftermath of the crisis, and have been unable to return to the rapid, and sustained, growth rates which they enjoyed for the decades from the mid-1960s to the mid-1990s. Some commentators have ascribed this failure to an inability on the part of governments in the region to tackle the problems which caused the crisis in the first place. Others argue that the rapid growth which occurred in the decades from the mid-1960s to the mid-1990s was the result of a fortunate combination of internal and external circumstances which is unlikely to occur again in the very different economic climate of the early Twenty-first Century. These commentators point to the rise of both China and India as formidable economic competitors for the ASEAN economies, both as locations for foreign investors and as exporters of a range of manufactured products. They argue that the ASEAN economies will have to accommodate themselves to the new economic giants emerging to the north and the west, and such accommodation is likely to be painful and present problems for most of the ASEAN economies with which their fragile political and administrative systems may be unable to cope.

Here it will be argued that there is some validity in both these arguments. There is certainly a strong case to be made that in both Indonesia and Thailand, the worst affected of the ASEAN economies, the lessons of 1997/98 have not been fully absorbed. Indeed there is still considerable controversy as to what those lessons really were. But in addition, there can be little doubt that the emergence of both China and India as important players in the global economy has presented all the ASEAN economies with both new opportunities and new challenges. How the countries of Southeast Asia respond to both the opportunities and challenges will determine their economic futures in coming decades. But before looking at these questions in greater detail, it will be useful to examine the economic progress of the ASEAN economies since the mid-1990s.

Economic Growth, Structural Change, Employment and Living Standards in ASEAN since 1995

It has been argued, not least by the Asian Development Bank in recent analyses, that the ASEAN economies as a group not only experienced growth collapses in 1997/98, but since then have managed only modest growth rates of Gross Domestic Product (GDP) compared with their pre-1995 achievements.[3] But the evidence suggests that the growth experience of the six largest ASEAN economies since 1995 has been very mixed. Several economies, including Vietnam, Singapore and Malaysia, have seen GDP increasing by more than sixty per cent between 1995 and 2006, which is much the same as in South Korea, or in Taiwan, an economy which was not severely affected by the 1997/98 problems (Table 1). Indeed Vietnam's growth since 1995 has been faster than in any of the other ASEAN economies, and almost as fast as that of China. Even the Philippines, long considered the poorest performer among the large ASEAN economies, has managed to grow by almost 60 per cent between 1995 and 2006, only slightly slower than Malaysia and South Korea. The two economies where the growth collapse was most severe, and where recovery has been slowest, have been Thailand and Indonesia. In Thailand, one of the fastest growing economies in the world between 1985 and 1995, growth of GDP between 1995 and 2006 was under 40 per cent; Indonesian growth was similar (Table 1).

So the real challenge is not to explain the 'failure' of the ASEAN countries as a group since the crisis, or indeed since the mid-1990s, but rather to explain the poor performance, relative to past trends, of two in particular. This is not to say that economies such as Malaysia and the Philippines have performed as well as they could have done after 1995. The Philippines did not suffer a growth collapse of the same magnitude as that in Malaysia, Thailand or Indonesia in 1998/99, but it has been plagued by political instability and a recalcitrant congress which has made the effective implementation of much-needed economic reforms in fiscal and trade policy extremely difficult. Per capita GDP in the

Philippines in 2005 was much lower than that in Thailand and Malaysia, or indeed China, although it is still higher than in Vietnam (Table 2). In Malaysia, there was a rapid recovery in growth between 1998 and 2000, but the slowdown in world demand for IT equipment in 2001 affected exports, and growth in that year was almost zero. In Singapore and Taiwan, which were also badly affected by the collapse in world demand for IT equipment, growth in 2001 was negative. Inevitably such open economies continue to be vulnerable to fluctuations in world demand for key exports.

Even allowing for slower growth after 1995, the 'first generation' Newly Industrialising Economies (NIEs), Singapore, Hong Kong, Taiwan and South Korea are still growing faster, in per capita terms, than the Organisation for Economic Co-operation and Development (OECD) average, and have much higher per capita GDP, and higher living standards, than any other Asian economy except Japan. In spite of the hype surrounding both China and India in recent years, both remain relatively low-income economies. India's per capita GDP, adjusted for purchasing power, was in 2005 slightly lower than that of Vietnam, and considerably lower than that of Indonesia, the Philippines and Thailand (Table 2). China's per capita GDP in 2005 was higher than all the ASEAN countries except Thailand, Malaysia, Singapore and Brunei, but still much lower than that of Taiwan and South Korea.[4] The gap between Hong Kong and mainland China remains very large indeed. Although these differences are smaller once allowance is made for the deviation between exchange rates and the actual purchasing power of currencies, they are still considerable.[5] Closing the very large gaps which still remain between rich and poor economies in Asia will continue to be a major challenge for most of the next century.

Another allegation which has been made by some commentators is that the slower post-crisis growth in Southeast Asia has led to 'de-industrialisation' in the sense that many manufacturing industries which grew rapidly in Singapore, Thailand, Indonesia and Malaysia since the late 1970s have either slowed or collapsed. As a consequence the proportion of the labour force employed in manufacturing has contracted. In fact the evidence for significant de-industrialisation is hardly persuasive. In both Thailand and Indonesia, the share of manufacturing in total GDP has increased in the ten years from 1995 to 2005 (Table 3). In both countries growth of manufactured exports was positive between 1997 and 2004, as indeed was the case in Singapore and Malaysia. In Thailand manufactured export growth accelerated to double digit figures between 2001 and 2004; this in turn contributed to the faster growth in output after 2001.[6]

The main structural change to emerge from the national income statistics in Thailand and Indonesia after 1995 has been on the expenditure side. Most of the ASEAN economies, with the exception of Vietnam and Cambodia have seen a fall in investment expenditures relative to GDP since the crisis.[7] David Green and other observers have argued that raising the level of investment to pre-crisis levels is crucial if growth is to accelerate. It would appear that the decline in investment by both public and private sectors is directly related to the crisis. In both Thailand and Indonesia, budgetary expenditures on capital works were squeezed to accommodate IMF (International Monetary Fund) demands for budgetary surpluses. In addition, especially in Indonesia, the budgetary cost of bank restructuring forced cutbacks in other expenditures, and the large government debt meant that the government was reluctant to borrow for infrastructure development.[8] Private sector investment in most parts of the region has been constrained by much tighter lending conditions imposed by banks, and many private firms which sent money abroad in 1997 and 1998 are still unwilling to repatriate it. Foreign direct investment also slowed, and indeed in Indonesia became negative in some years. Although Indonesia was more severely affected than other economies, the same factors negatively affected investment in most parts of the region between 1997 and 2004.

But would raising investment alone be enough to accelerate growth in the future? In most parts of the region there is a need to improve investment productivity by ensuring that it is directed to projects with the highest returns, whether in the public or the private sector. In spite of the improvements which have occurred in the banking sector, there is ample evidence that banks in Southeast Asia are still unwilling to function as efficient intermediaries between savers and investors. Various suggestions have been made for improving the efficiency of banks in the region but reforms are likely to take years, or decades, to have much impact. Similarly, in spite of much talk about reform of corporate governance, progress has been slow in most parts of the region. While the Washington-based international organisations tend to favour the so-called 'Anglo-American' business model, it has been argued that other models including the family-based firm have performed well in many parts of Asia. I return to this point below.

There have also been changes in employment and unemployment, especially in Indonesia, where employment in some labour-intensive sectors of manufacturing such as textiles, clothing and footwear declined after 2000, although it is unclear whether this was the result of the crisis, or of other problems affecting Indonesian manufactured exports including greater competition from Vietnam and China. These problems are addressed in more detail below. There has been little change in the proportion of the total labour force employed in agriculture, manufacturing and services in Indonesia between 1996/97 and 2004/5, although it has been argued that there has been a shift in total employment from formal to informal activities.[9] What has caused considerable concern in Indonesia is the rise in rates of open unemployment after 1995, together with a fall in labour force participation rates, especially among women workers. In 2005, open unemployment was estimated to be 10.3 per cent of the total labour force, although there was a slight fall in 2006. Open unemployment was especially high in the 15-24 age groups and among senior high school graduates.[10]

How much of the increase in unemployment since the mid-1990s in Indonesia has been due to slower growth and how much to policies including higher minimum wages and more intensive regulation of labour markets? This remains a debated issue. It has been argued that minimum wages have led to higher unemployment in urban areas. In Thailand where labour markets are less regulated, unemployment rose in the immediate aftermath of the crisis but fell again quite rapidly; by the third quarter of 2001 open unemployment was officially estimated to be only 2.6 per cent.[11] As in Indonesia, unemployment in Thailand tended to be higher among the better educated; in 2001 the highest rates were found among graduates from upper secondary and tertiary institutions. Enrolments at both secondary and tertiary institutions increased rapidly in Thailand over the 1990s and after 1998 many graduates clearly experienced difficulty in finding the kind of jobs to which they felt their education entitled them.

What impact did the crisis and the subsequent slow recovery have on living standards? In the immediate aftermath of the growth collapses in both Indonesia and Thailand, many predicted a sharp increase in the headcount measure of poverty (the percentage of the population spending less than the official poverty line). Such an increase did indeed happen.[12] In the cases of Thailand, Medhi Krongkaew and Nanak Kakwani estimated that the headcount measure of Thailand rose from 11.4 per cent in 1996 to 16.2 per cent in 2000.[13] Peter Warr argued that there was a sharp decline after 2000, and by 2002 the headcount measure was lower than at any point during the 1990s.[14] A similar rise and fall also occurred in Indonesia. The official estimates of the headcount measure of poverty published by the Central Board of Statistics show an increase between 1996 and 1999 (from 17.7 per cent to 23.5 per cent) and then a decline to just under 16 per cent by 2005.[15] But because of population growth the absolute numbers below the official poverty line were still slightly higher in 2005 than in 1996 (35.1 million compared with 34.5 million).[16]

In an attempt to come up with an internationally-comparable poverty line, the World Bank for a number of years used the 'dollar a day' and 'two dollars a day' measures. According to estimates published in 2006, most of the ASEAN economies now have fewer than 20 per cent of their populations below the dollar a day poverty line; only Cambodia and Laos are above 20 per cent (Table 4). Perhaps surprisingly, given that their per capita GDP is lower than China's, the proportion of the population below the dollar a day measure in both the Philippines and Indonesia was estimated by the World Bank to have been slightly lower than in China at the end of the Twentieth Century, although the proportion below the two dollar a day measure was higher.[17] This suggests that, while both Indonesia and the Philippines, as well as Thailand, made considerable progress towards eliminating extreme poverty during the last part of the Twentieth Century, many households in all these countries were still living below a fairly basic level.[18] Even in relatively prosperous Malaysia, the World Bank estimated that in 1997 around nine per cent of the population was still below the two dollar a day level.[19]

Most ASEAN countries have experienced a rise in life expectancies during the last three decades of the

Twentieth Century, and also a rise in school attendance and in adult literacy. By the end of the Twentieth Century, most countries in the region had adult literacy rates of around 90 per cent, which was much the same as in China. Life expectancies for women were also much the same as in China in most ASEAN countries; the main exceptions being Myanmar, Cambodia and Laos (Table 4). In Thailand and Indonesia, the proportion of the population over 15 with upper secondary or tertiary education was also roughly similar to China in 2000, although both countries had a lower proportion of the population with lower secondary education (Table 5). This reflects the fact that the goal of universal nine-year education was adopted rather later in both Thailand and Indonesia than in China. It is also probable that the growth collapses in 1998 and the slow recovery in both Thailand and Indonesia have had an adverse impact on school enrolments at both the secondary and tertiary levels, especially among lower income groups. Evidence for Indonesia in 2003 indicates much higher enrolments among young people from the top 20 per cent of the expenditure distribution at both these levels, with a strong bias to urban areas (Table 6). In most parts of Southeast Asia, educational participation beyond primary level is still very much influenced by family income and location.

There can be little doubt that the impact of the slower growth in both Thailand and Indonesia in the decade 1995-2005 had a serious impact on incomes and living standards, and especially in Indonesia recovery has been slow. While few now dispute that there was a sharp decline in poverty in Indonesia in the two decades from 1976 to 1996, the evidence indicates that there has been little change in the proportion of the population below the official poverty line between 1996 and 2006, and an increase in the absolute numbers of the poor. While many non-poor in Indonesia, and in other parts of the region, also suffered income declines after 1997, the impact of the crisis was most severe on the most vulnerable. This is no doubt one reason why many Indonesians feel that the promise of reform in the aftermath of Soeharto's departure from office has yielded disappointing results. I turn now to look in more detail at the implementation of reform in the post-crisis period in Southeast Asia.

Tackling Domestic Problems in the Aftermath of the Crisis

The 'Asian Crisis' of 1997/98 spawned a very large literature, which has continued to expand to the present. While some consensus has emerged about the causes of the crisis, there is still considerable debate about particular issues. There are also ongoing debates about the policies adopted by different countries in the aftermath of the crisis, and especially about the policies adopted by the Prime Minister Mahathir Mohamad's government in Malaysia in the latter part of 1998. The area where there is probably greatest consensus is over the cause of the problems in Thailand, which led to the decision to float the baht in early July 1997. By 1996 a number of academic commentators, as well as the international financial press, were pointing to the sharp slowdown in Thai export performance, and in economic growth in 1996, and arguing that the policy of pegging the baht to the dollar would have to be modified.[20] Some also argued that the combination of the pegged exchange rate and the open capital account had rendered monetary policy useless as a tool of domestic economic stabilisation, and this had led to the 'asset bubble' which had driven up prices of both equities and real estate since the early 1990s.

Exactly why the Bank of Thailand (BOT) was so slow to react to the problems which were very clear by the mid-1990s, including the deteriorating foreign exchange situation, has been the subject of much discussion. There seems to be little doubt that the institution had become heavily politicised in the early 1990s.[21] What had been one of the more independent and technocratic central banks in the region was increasingly prone to political interference; in addition some highly qualified staff had moved to the private sector and less competent officials were in charge of managing foreign exchange policy.[22] Given that so many banks and corporate enterprises in Thailand had borrowed heavily abroad in dollars, or other foreign currencies, there was considerable pressure on the BOT from domestic banks, finance companies and other firms not to allow the exchange rate to float. As capital outflow accelerated, the BOT used its reserves to buy baht in the hope of stabilising the market. By mid-1997 it was clear that this policy was no longer viable. Reserves had been exhausted and there was little alternative but to float the baht, and ask the IMF for emergency balance-of-payments assistance.

Many commentators have subsequently pointed out that if Thailand had not 'prematurely' liberalised the capital account by establishing the Bangkok International Banking Facility (BIBF) in 1993, the Thai crisis could have been contained and the damaging contagion to other parts of Asia would not have occurred. Stiglitz has argued that 'capital account liberalisation was pushed on these countries in the late eighties and early nineties', and this was the 'single most important factor leading to the crisis'.[23] In fact in the Thai case, it would appear that, far from being pushed on the Thai government from outside, the BIBF was enthusiastically supported by the politically powerful Bangkok banking establishment, who wanted to see Bangkok become a regional banking centre to rival Singapore.[24] Those Thai economists, of whom there was a not inconsiderable number, who were worried about the loss of monetary control which inevitably resulted from the liberalisation of the capital account in the context of a pegged exchange rate, were sidelined and ignored.[25]

Elsewhere in Southeast Asia there were considerable differences in the timing of capital account liberalisation. In Indonesia, the relatively new government of President Soeharto implemented a policy of a fully convertible exchange rate in 1970, and at the same time removed most controls on the import and export of capital although foreign investors wishing to invest in Indonesia had to go through a government agency in order to get the necessary licenses. The removal of controls on capital export was motivated by the realisation that controls in the first two decades of independence had worked badly and only led to corruption.[26] Given the *de facto* integration of Indonesia with capital markets in Singapore and Hong Kong, it was argued that it was better to remove controls so that most capital flows, especially between Chinese businesses, would be legal and transparent. The Indonesian experience was unusual in that it did not follow the sequence of liberalisation advocated by most authorities according to which the liberalisation of the capital account should follow other measures such as removal of credit and interest rate controls and reduction of controls on commodity exports and imports.[27]

Until the mid-1990s most observers considered that the Indonesian policy, although atypical, had been reasonably successful. Compared with the bold decision to remove most controls on the export of capital in 1970, liberalisation of the domestic financial system proceeded quite slowly and it was not until 1983 that the Indonesian government removed bank credit ceilings for both state and private banks, and also deregulated interest rates for state banks. The result was a rapid expansion in bank lending especially from private banks, and a convergence in interest rates between state and private banks. These trends continued after 1988, when the PAKTO reforms allowed the establishment of new banks, and an increase in branches for existing private banks. The combined impact of these reforms was a considerable increase in the ratio of M2 (coins, notes, demand, savings and time deposits) to GDP.[28] Senior government officials admitted that the more liberal domestic financial system, combined with the open capital account, and the policy of slowly depreciating the nominal value of the rupiah, made domestic monetary management more difficult. A particular difficulty in the Indonesian context was the instability of expectations about the exchange rate which not infrequently triggered large capital outflows.[29]

The Indonesian approach to financial reform was certainly much more of a high wire act than that in Malaysia, where the sequencing of reforms was more conventional, and the overall approach to financial liberalisation more cautious.[30] In contrast to Indonesia, the Malaysian central bank (Bank Negara Malaysia) tended to allow financial deregulation to proceed only as rapidly as effective regulatory mechanisms could be put in place. During the 1980s considerable liberalisation of the current account preceded liberalisation of the capital account. Although by the early 1990s few controls remained on the export of capital, and controls on foreign borrowing by domestic residents and companies were loosened, the monetary authorities were far from doctrinaire in their approach to the capital account and had introduced temporary capital controls in early 1994 after a sudden reversal of earlier large portfolio inflows.[31] Given this history, it was not difficult for the central bank to reimpose controls in 1998, although the decision was controversial, and prompted the resignation of several senior officials in Bank Negara Malaysia.

Thus while Stiglitz is simply wrong in his assertion that capital account liberalisation was forced on Thailand, Indonesia and Malaysia in the 1980s by outside influences, it was true that by the mid-1990s all three countries had quite open and deregulated financial systems, including open capital accounts. By 1996, signs of vulnerability were evident, although in a climate of sustained growth of GDP, few were paying attention. Three aspects of financial vulnerability have subsequently been identified; falling reserves relative to the stock of mobile capital, a rapid growth in the ratio of private sector credit to GDP and an appreciation of the real exchange rate.[32] The appreciation of the exchange rate was probably one factor behind the increased capital flight in the years from 1993 to 1995, particularly in Thailand and Indonesia.[33] In both countries, large companies owned by Thais and Indonesians of Chinese descent were investing in other parts of Asia, especially in China, where exchange rate policy favoured the rapid expansion of labour-intensive traded goods industries. Domestic lending, especially in Thailand and Malaysia, was increasingly concentrated in non-traded sectors, with a strong bias towards real estate.[34]

But even in a climate of increased volatility, most external observers in the early and mid- 1990s felt that the financial systems in the ASEAN region could cope, without catastrophic capital flight, and financial collapse. Even after the problems in Thailand had become the subject of several critical reviews in the international financial press in the latter part of 1996, assessments of economic conditions in the other ASEAN economies remained positive.[35] Natasha Hamilton-Hart has pointed out that there were at least three favourable reports on the Indonesian economy by major banks and ratings agencies in late 1996 and early 1997, and very bullish articles were also published in the regional financial press.[36] This was in spite of signs of growing political unrest and ethnic and religious violence, both in Java and in West Kalimantan. Right up until the decision to allow the rupiah to float freely in August 1997, the opinion of most observers was that the fundamentals in Indonesia were sound, and the problems in Thailand, while serious, would not be contagious.

What went wrong? Given the rapid currency depreciation and massive outflows of capital which did occur in 1997 and 1998, the severe growth collapses in 1998 and the subsequent slower growth, it is hardly surprising that several commentators have blamed the open capital account and 'premature' financial deregulation as the main causal factors. In one sense this is little more than a statement of the obvious; if there had been effective capital controls in Thailand or Indonesia in the early and mid-1990s, these would have prevented the very large capital outflows which occurred.[37] Thus in Thailand there would have been less need for the regime of high interest rates and fiscal contraction implemented after July 1997 in order to stem the capital outflow. It is possible that there would still have been a slowdown in growth due to the diversion of investment into the domestic non-traded sector, but the severe growth collapse would probably have been avoided. While the claim that the re-imposition of capital controls in Malaysia was the main reason for the faster recovery in that economy may be exaggerated, capital controls certainly made it easier for the Malaysian government to adopt fiscal and monetary policies which stimulated faster growth.

But could capital controls have worked in the political climate which prevailed in Indonesia and Thailand in the 1980s and 1990s? There can be little doubt that in Thailand and Indonesia powerful business interests wanted an open capital account, and would have opposed any attempt by government to re-impose capital controls. Many businesses throughout Southeast Asia in the early 1990s found it very easy to borrow in foreign currencies in order to benefit from lower interest rates in currencies such as the dollar and the yen.[38] In addition, large conglomerates, especially those owned by citizens of Chinese descent, wanted to diversify their businesses into other parts of Asia, especially China. In Indonesia businesses controlled by indigenous Indonesians with close family ties to Soeharto and other political leaders were uncertain about what sort of regime would emerge in the post-Soeharto era, and had begun to shift funds abroad as a political and economic hedge well before the Thai decision to float the baht. In early 1998, as the rupiah declined to less than 20 per cent of its mid-1997 value against the dollar, Soeharto's family and their business associates supported the establishment of a currency board which would have permitted free capital movements at a pegged exchange rate. Most observers saw this as little more than a cynical ploy to allow businesses and individuals connected to Soeharto to move money off-shore at a favourable exchange rate, but the fact that it was seriously advocated by members of Soeharto's family indicates that any attempt to impose capital controls at that time would have been frustrated.[39]

Even after the departure of Soeharto in May 1998, there was little change in Indonesian government policy towards the exchange rate and capital controls. In part this reflected the influence of the IMF, but in addition there seems to have been a strong bias in both the government and the business sector against the imposition of capital controls. This was probably due to a realisation that, in spite of legislation giving it greater independence, Bank Indonesia was still vulnerable to political interference which would have made effective implementation of such controls impossible. In the years from 1999 to 2004 most emphasis was on restructuring the devastated banking system. There can be little doubt that the measures initially adopted by the authorities in late 1997 and early 1998 to cope with the emerging problems in the banking system aggravated the situation. The introduction of a blanket guarantee for all bank deposits was delayed until January 1998, by which time many people had shifted their savings to state banks or to branches of foreign banks, or moved them off-shore. Many of the private banks which had expanded rapidly after the 1988 reforms were bankrupt through a combination of non-performing loans and the flight of deposits. The Indonesian Bank Restructuring Authority (IBRA) which was established in 1998 was not given a clear legal mandate for over a year, and its work was continually hampered by political interference and accusations of corruption.

In spite of these problems, some progress was made in bank restructuring in Indonesia, and by 2004 government shares in the nationalised and re-capitalised banks had been largely sold off.[40] By the end of 2003, numbers of commercial banks had been reduced to 138 from a pre-crisis level of 239, the capital/asset ratio had returned to pre-crisis levels, and the gross non-performing loan ratio had fallen to 8.1 per cent, which was lower than the pre-crisis level.[41] The main factor leading to the improvement in the capital asset ratio was the huge injection of government money, amounting to 52 per cent of GDP in 2000. But bank lending remained at a much lower level, relative to nominal GDP, than before the crisis. This reflected the slow pace of economic growth between 1998 and 2003, the low confidence in the business sector, and the stricter risk management procedures imposed by banks on clients after the crisis. IBRA ultimately assumed ownership rights over bank assets with a face value of Rp 534 trillion, but many of them turned out to be worthless. Although IBRA was tasked with extracting as much value as possible from these assets, it would appear that it realised less than 30 per cent of their nominal value by the time the agency was dissolved in 2004.[42]

The cost to the Indonesian government, and to the taxpayer, of bank restructuring was enormous. IMF conditions imposed on the government included a ceiling on budget deficits. Thus there was little option, as budgetary expenditures on bank restructuring increased, but to reduce expenditure on other heads of expenditure including infrastructure and education.[43] In Thailand, the government of Chuan Leekpai tried to avoid an Indonesian-type outcome by adopting a more 'market-based' approach to the problems of the banks and the corporate sector. Emphasis was put on forcing insolvent companies into bankruptcy procedures, or to make asset sales to pay off debt. It refused to buy out the bad loans of the banks, thus forcing them to tackle the problem directly. Although this minimised the cost to government the inevitable consequence was that banks, rather than write down their debts, tried to re-schedule loans to clients. This meant that many firms were still saddled with large debts and could not take out new loans to finance expansion, even when good business opportunities were available. This certainly impeded the pace of recovery, and caused widespread anger in the business community.[44] When the Chuan government fell in 2001, the new Thaksin Shinawatra government announced that it would establish an asset management company (TAMC) to buy out the bad loans from banks.[45] It was expected that this would assist in increasing bank lending, although the TAMC, like IBRA, did not have a good track record in recovering bad debts from the corporate sector.

The activities of IBRA were compromised from the beginning by the willingness of a number of large Indonesian conglomerates to sacrifice their banks in order to preserve their corporate assets, both on-shore and off-shore.[46] Most of the large conglomerates owned banks, but they were, for the most part, subsidiary to their other business activities. Much of their lending was to companies within the conglomerate, or to enterprises at least partially owned by business people associated with the conglomerate.[47] The Indonesian corporate sector was characterised by a high degree of concentration, even compared with the Philippines and Thailand, let alone South Korea, Hong Kong, Singapore and Malaysia.[48] This concentration was also reflected in private bank ownership and in the rescue efforts of Bank Indonesia in late 1997 and early 1998. The controversial liquidity credits which were granted by Bank Indonesia in late 1997 and early 1998 flowed mainly to private banks, and particularly to three private banks, each associated with politically influential conglomerates. They were Bank Central Asia, Bank Danamon and Bank Dagang Nasional Indonesia. The liquidity credits were unsecured, with only personal guarantees provided by their owners. Later investigations by the Supreme Audit Board showed that irregular practices had dominated the administration of the liquidity credits, with a large proportion being mis-used.[49]

In spite of the serious problems which most of the large conglomerates, together with many smaller businesses, faced in the aftermath of the crisis throughout Southeast Asia, the majority continued to operate, although many were forced to divest themselves of at least some of their assets to settle outstanding loans with banks. But the divestment process was often far from transparent, and, especially in Indonesia, there were examples of businesses being purchased by groups which were hardly arms-length from the conglomerate. In addition several conglomerates in Indonesia were able to use their assets there to obtain new loans abroad. Perhaps the most egregious example of this was the Sinar Mas conglomerate in Indonesia which through an affiliated company, APP, borrowed heavily in the United

States and Asia to finance the expansion of its pulp and paper businesses in China and elsewhere. This continued after 1997, in spite of the fact that the bank linked to Sinar Mas had granted large loans to APP which APP refused to pay back once the bank had been taken over by IBRA. It became clear that IBRA itself was hardly acting as an independent honest broker in the Sinar Mas-APP affair, but permitted the sale of assets at discounted prices to entities suspected of being linked to Sinar Mas.[50]

The Sinar Mas-APP case, and others like it, raised broader problems of corporate governance which were also taken up after the crisis by international agencies, both in Indonesia and Thailand. Before 1997 this was not an issue which was given much attention; most commentators believed that even if firms were badly managed and ran into cash flow difficulties, their problems could be sorted out in a context of dense business networks, and of rapid economic growth.[51] Bankruptcy legislation existed in most parts of ASEAN; usually the legislation was based on that of the former colonial power. But given the corruption and inefficiencies in the legal system, there was little incentive to use it. Faced with widespread corporate collapse in 1998/99, it was clear that more effective procedures would have to be put in place, but there was little agreement on how this should be done. The Bretton Woods institutions tended to blame the problems in the corporate sector in Indonesia, Thailand and Malaysia on the ownership structure of many large firms, where even in publicly-listed companies, families retained control over most key decisions and minority shareholders had little power. But although there was some evidence that the structure of ownership was changing after the crisis, particularly in Indonesia, there was considerable debate about the effect of these changes on firm performance.[52]

The ongoing problems with corporate restructuring in Indonesia and the publicity given to the activities of IBRA led many Indonesians to suspect that, in spite of the political changes which took place in the wake of Soeharto's departure from office, the problems of 'corruption, collusion and nepotism' which had provoked student protests in 1998, had not gone away. Powerful groups within the parliament, and in the governments of the three presidents who succeeded Soeharto in quick succession between 1998 and 2001, were apparently able to influence the decisions of IBRA and other government agencies, including the courts, in favour of business groups associated with the Soeharto era. These perceptions were shared by domestic and foreign business groups, and showed up in international league tables of corruption and governance. The governance 'league table' constructed by World Bank economists shows that the control of corruption in Indonesia actually deteriorated in Indonesia between 1996 and 2005. This was in spite of the improvement in 'voice and accountability' which had occurred (Table 7). There was also some deterioration in Malaysia, the Philippines and Vietnam over these years, although in 2005 Indonesia was ranked lower in terms of control of corruption, and in terms of government effectiveness, than any other ASEAN country except Laos, Cambodia and Myanmar.

The lesson from Table 7 appears to be that a move towards a more open and 'accountable' political system is not automatically associated with improvements in either the ability of government agencies to conduct their operations in a reasonably clean and efficient way, or in the extent of corruption, at least as this is measured by the World Bank. In Indonesia since the departure of Soeharto, problems of effective delivery of government services have been complicated by the move towards a more decentralised system of government which gives more responsibility, especially regarding delivery of basic services such as health and education, to lower levels of government. While it is still too early to reach firm conclusions on how well, or badly, the decentralisation legislation is working in practice, the devolution of responsibility does mean that local officials have more scope for using funds for personal enrichment. In addition there are fears that decentralisation is a major factor in the decline in investment in Indonesia, although here too it seems premature to reach strong conclusions. But in some sectors, such as mining, there is evidence that decentralisation has increased uncertainty in doing business in particular localities.[53]

From the above discussion, it seems legitimate to conclude that, whatever view is taken about the causes of the 1997/98 crisis, lessons have not been learnt. Those who argue that the fundamental problem was 'premature' liberalisation of the capital account, or of the domestic financial system, can point out that no government in the region except Malaysia re-imposed capital controls, and indeed Malaysia has removed most of those imposed in 1998. The main effect of the crisis, as far as capital controls go, is that those economies such as Vietnam, which had controls prior to the crisis have been understandably reluctant to abandon them. The Thai government did try to impose a tax on inward flows of portfolio investment in December 2006, apparently to prevent an appreciation of the baht, which occurred anyway. The main effect of the Thai move was to further depress business confidence, already shaken by the coup against Thaksin. Malaysia re-floated the ringgit after seven years of operating on a pegged rate in 2005; the result has been an appreciation against the dollar. From 2005, all the main ASEAN currencies have been 'floating', albeit with some government intervention.[54] Most have seen some appreciation against the dollar.[55]

Those who viewed the 'vulnerability' of the Southeast Asian economies as the result of corruption and cronyism have to confront the evidence that Indonesia in particular has apparently made little progress in dealing with these problems. The IMF argued that during the 1990s, 'there emerged a creeping return to restrictive business practices and rent-seeking opportunities for the President's family and well-connected businessmen, with a corresponding weakening of regulatory and supervisory controls'.[56] Many Indonesians would argue that, in spite of the departure of Soeharto and the emergence after 2004 of a president with a strong direct mandate from the electorate, progress towards eliminating these practices has been very slow. In addition, in both Indonesia and Thailand, there seems to be substantial agreement that the old methods of macro-economic management, which underpinned rapid economic growth in the three decades from the mid-1960s to the mid-1990s, have now fractured. To the extent that new processes of decision-making are emerging, they involve compromise with a diverse range of power bases in parliament, political parties, religious groups, and the regions as well as with an array of Non-Governmental Organisations (NGOs). This inevitably slows down decision-making and creates an impression of an executive branch that is indecisive and not infrequently venal.

The International Environment

The process of economic recovery in the ASEAN countries since 1998 has had to take place in a rapidly changing regional and international context. The major economies of Southeast Asia developed during the colonial era, and especially in the decades from 1870 to 1930, as exporters of a narrow range of tropical agricultural products and minerals. Their share of all exports from all tropical countries increased rapidly until by 1937 they accounted for almost one third of all such exports.[57] After 1945, this percentage declined, reflecting the political and economic difficulties which a number of Southeast Asian countries experienced in the transition to independence and the immediate post-independence years. But over the last quarter of the Twentieth Century exports from Southeast Asia surged again; between 1975 and 2001, the share of the ASEAN countries in global trade increased from 2.7 to 6.3 per cent.[58] This was mainly the result of rapid export diversification into a range of manufactured products, including textiles, garments, footwear, and electronics.

Although the export performance of the ASEAN countries since 1975 looks impressive in world terms, it is less dramatic than that of China. In 1985, exports from China were (in dollar terms) less than half those from the ASEAN countries; by 2001 they had more than caught up and amounted to 6.5 per cent of world exports.[59] Between 1996 and 2006, exports from China grew much more rapidly than from the ASEAN region; by 2006, exports from China were around 26 per cent higher than the ASEAN total (Table 8). Furthermore, much of the growth in exports in ASEAN since 1985 has come from just three countries: Singapore, Malaysia and Thailand. These three economies accounted for over 70 per cent of the growth in ASEAN exports between 1985 and 2001; Singapore alone accounted for around one third of the increment in exports from ASEAN between 1996 and 2006.[60] Indonesia whose exports, in dollar terms, were larger than any other Southeast Asian economy in 1985 experienced slower growth over the last two decades of the Twentieth Century than most other countries in the region. This reflected the fall in both value and volume of its oil exports, as well as slower growth of non-oil exports from the mid-1990s onwards. The last part of the Twentieth Century saw a rapid growth in exports from Vietnam, Laos and Cambodia but from a very low base, so that these three countries still only accounted for around six per cent of total ASEAN exports in 2006.

In Singapore, Malaysia, Thailand, Indonesia and the Philippines, the share of total exports going to, and imports sourced from, other parts of East and Southeast Asia (excluding Japan) increased over the years from 1985 to 2001.[61] This was partly the result of increased trade with China, and partly the result of increased trade within the ASEAN region. By the early Twenty-first Century, China had become an important trading partner with ASEAN. Siow-Yue Chia estimated that in 2003 China accounted for 6.7 per cent of total ASEAN exports and 7.4 per cent of China's imports were sourced from ASEAN.[62] About 80 per cent of total ASEAN exports to China were manufactures (especially electrical equipment and other machinery), mineral fuels and oils, organic chemicals and plastics, vegetable oils and wood products.[63] Since 1998, there has also been an increase in intra-ASEAN trade as a share of total ASEAN trade, from around 21 per cent to over 25 per cent.[64] The growth of intra-ASEAN trade, coupled with the growth in trade with China and other countries in Asia have provoked discussions of new regional economic institutions in the region. I return to this topic below.

China's rapid rise as an exporter of manufactured exports has inevitably given rise to fears in the ASEAN economies, as well as elsewhere, that their own manufactured exports will not be able to compete with those from China in important markets such as the United States, the European Union (EU) and Japan. China's wage rates are thought to be much lower than in most parts of Southeast Asia; United Nations Conference on Trade and Development (UNCTAD) data indicate that they are only about one quarter of those in Malaysia and half those in Indonesia, although per capita GDP is lower in Indonesia than in China.[65] It is often argued that labour laws are either lax or non-existent in most parts of China, and workers work long hours, often with no overtime pay. This can be contrasted with Indonesia, where labour unions have become more powerful since the end of the Soeharto era, and formal labour markets have become more tightly regulated.

Empirical studies suggest that in the latter part of the 1990s, the ASEAN Five (Indonesia, Malaysia, the Philippines, Thailand and Singapore) did lose market share to China in both the Japanese and the American markets. David Holst and John Weiss found that for large categories of ASEAN exports such as electronics and electrical and engineering products, there was 'a consistent pattern of loss of competitiveness' in the sense that relative market share declined, although the absolute value of exports grew.[66] For some other categories of exports, including primary products, resource-based manufactures and textiles, garments and footwear, there was an absolute decline in ASEAN exports to both Japan and the United States. Of course not all of this decline would have been due to competition from China, but in export categories such as textiles, garments and footwear most of it would have been. Holst and Weiss argued that the combined value of the loss in market share for the ASEAN Five was not compensated by increased exports to China. In fact they estimate that the net export gain to China was only about 20 per cent of the loss in market share in the United States and Japan, although they pointed out that in Thailand and Malaysia, there were 'the strongest signs' of a compensating effect.

Other authors have reached more positive conclusions about the impact of China on the ASEAN economies. For example Francis Ng and Alexander Yeats have argued:

> ...evidence based on intra-industry trade ratios, or statistics on international production sharing, show economic linkages and the interdependence of East Asian economies have considerably strengthened. Furthermore, the export and import profiles of East Asian countries have been changing in directions that increase complementarity which further increases the potential for intra-regional trade. China's emergence has been a major positive influence on the region.[67]

While this argument seems to be at odds with the findings of Holst and Weiss, it is reinforced by the evidence that at least some ASEAN economies have managed to both increase exports to China, and successfully compete with China in third markets, particularly in products such as hard disk drives and other electronics, and in automobiles and parts. Sanjaya Lall pointed out that in 1998, 'high technology' exports accounted for a substantial share (over half) of total manufactured exports from the Philippines, Malaysia and Singapore.[68] In all countries these exports originated from local branches of multi-nationals, although local content was important in Singapore. Some authors (for example Prema-Chandra Athukorala) have argued that the rather poor performance of Indonesia since 1998 in manufactured exports has much more to do with domestic policies than with competition from China.[69] While he concedes that the emergence of China has 'made life more challenging' for exporters from Indonesia he blames supply-side factors including the regulatory regime and poor infrastructure for many of Indonesia's problems.[70]

Since the crisis there has been much talk of enhanced co-operation between Asian economies. Within ASEAN there has been a revived attempt to reduce trade barriers within the region, as set out in the ASEAN Free Trade Area (AFTA) agreement of the early 1990s.[71] There is also now a commitment to an ASEAN Economic Community (AEC) by 2015, five years ahead of the original goal. This is a serious initiative to remove remaining barriers to trade in both goods and services, as well as encourage freer flows of capital and skilled (but not unskilled) labour. There can be no doubt that this is driven by a realisation that, in order to compete with China, the ASEAN countries must move towards a genuine economic union of more than 550 million people. ASEAN countries are also reaching out to other parts of the Asian region, in addition to closer economic union within ASEAN. A Framework Agreement signed in 2002 committed the ASEAN-6 to a free trade area with China by 2010, with Cambodia, Myanmar, Laos and Vietnam joining in 2015.[72] Some of the more developed ASEAN economies, especially Singapore, Thailand and Malaysia, are already signing bilateral trade deals with other countries in Asia, including China and Japan.

Some economists view the 'noodle bowl' of bilateral deals with some alarm, and argue that their effect will be to divert rather than create trade, although there is as yet not much evidence of discriminatory liberalisation.[73] There are certainly fears among some ASEAN countries that freer trade with China will lead to more competition from cheap Chinese manufactures and thus place domestic industries such as textiles and garments under more pressure. To allay these fears, the ASEAN-China Expert Group has produced results from a modelling exercise which shows that some of the poorer ASEAN economies, such as Indonesia and Vietnam will benefit from freer trade with China, in that both exports and GDP will increase. The simulation model also indicated that a free trade area would lead to some reduction in trade with the rest of the world for both ASEAN and China.[74] Such an outcome may well make intra-Asian trade deals politically acceptable in the United States and the EU, if not within Asia itself.

There has also been much discussion within Asia since the crisis about increased monetary co-operation. In Chiengmai in May 2000, the ASEAN plus 3 (China, Korea and Japan) group agreed to establish a network of bilateral swaps, for countries facing short-term pressures in the foreign exchange market. Some commentators hailed this as a first step towards a regional system of currency pegs, an East Asian Monetary Fund, and ultimately a common currency. There is little doubt that the Chiengmai Imitative (CMI) reflected a profound sense of anger and betrayal among those economies most damaged by the 1997/98 crisis towards the IMF and the World Bank which had failed to anticipate the crisis, and indeed possibly helped to precipitate it by over-hyping the achievements of countries such as Korea, Thailand,

Indonesia and Malaysia prior to 1997. The IMF was also criticised for making a bad situation worse by imposing very stringent fiscal and monetary conditions on the three countries which had sought their help.

In addition the CMI reflected quite widespread views in several Asian countries that the system of floating exchange rates, which had emerged after the crisis, was inherently unstable and indeed incompatible with the export and investment-led development model pioneered by Japan, which had served many Asian economies well in the last four decades of the Twentieth Century. But sceptics have pointed out that the prevailing economic and political conditions in the ASEAN plus 3 countries make it unlikely that closer monetary integration will be achieved in the immediate future. The countries are very heterogeneous in terms of per capita GDP and other development indicators, and in spite of the growth in intra-regional trade over the last 15 years, their trade is still less integrated than the EU.[75] In addition it has been argued that the ASEAN plus 3 governments have little real appetite for closer integration, and most remain deeply suspicious of all supra-national institutions.[76] As memories of the 1997/98 debacle fade, and as governments change, either through the ballot box or by other means, it seems unlikely that much real progress towards economic integration will be achieved.

A Summing Up

The first conclusion relates to the arguments that the major Southeast Asian economies, with the exception of Vietnam, have not managed to return to the growth rates achieved over the decades previous to the crisis. While this is true of both Thailand and Indonesia, the evidence is less clearcut for other ASEAN countries. Vietnam has powered ahead in the decade since 1995, and the Philippines has grown much faster since 1995 than over the 1980s. To the extent that both Singapore and Malaysia grew more slowly after 1995, the reason is only partly to be found in the consequences of the crisis. Demand for their principal exports fell in 2001 as a result of the collapse of the dot.com boom in the USA. In several ASEAN economies, especially the Philippines and Indonesia, the rapid growth of Chinese exports has undermined their competitiveness in markets such as the USA and Japan, especially for the traditional labour-intensive products. There can be little doubt that China has been exploiting its large reserves of cheap labour to out-compete labour-intensive exports from Southeast Asia. This may of course change in the future as new patterns of comparative advantage emerge in both China and ASEAN, and as trade between the two increases.

A second conclusion relates to the complex issue of corruption and government efficiency. The Asian Development Bank has given much publicity to estimates of the World Bank which show that several performance indicators relating to governance and control of corruption in the major Southeast Asian economies have deteriorated since 1996.[77] While this is correct, it should be noted that the indicators relating to voice and accountability, government effectiveness and control of corruption all deteriorated in China as well over this period. In 2005, China was ranked lower than five ASEAN countries in terms of control of corruption, including Thailand and the Philippines; its score was roughly equal to that of Vietnam (Table 7). This does not appear to have negatively affected growth in either China or Vietnam, and it would seem that governance indicators by themselves are not always reliable predictors of economic performance.

The third conclusion relates to changing patterns of comparative advantage, both within the East Asian region, and in the wider global economy. Many industrialists and worker organisations in the ASEAN countries view China's ambitions in the region with distrust; some would even argue that China's aim is to re-impose a 'colonial' trade pattern on the ASEAN countries, whereby the ASEAN economies would export raw materials and processed agricultural products to China in return for manufactures. While such a pattern of trade may be emerging in some cases, there is evidence that the more developed ASEAN economies such as Singapore, Malaysia and Thailand are exporting a range of manufactures, including components, to China, in return for other manufactures. Such trade is likely to continue to expand. Whether the other ASEAN economies can also become part of these growing networks depends on the investment by foreign multinationals and local counterparts, which in turn will depend on the availability of skilled labour, better infrastructure and administration, and more domestic expenditures on research and development. It has been argued that some Southeast Asian countries such as Indonesia 'are not participating vigorously in regional production networks and are weak in intermediate goods exports'.[78] This is due to weaknesses in infrastructure, logistics and education. Although both Indonesia and Thailand have made considerable progress in expanding educational enrolments over the past two decades, they still lag behind China, especially in the proportion of the population with primary education or less. In 2000, this was over 80 per cent in Thailand and over 60 per cent in Indonesia compared with 42 per cent in China, and only 24 per cent in Taiwan (Table 5).

A fourth conclusion relates to the role of regional trading arrangements and moves towards closer financial integration, both within ASEAN and in the wider East Asian context. There has certainly been a proliferation of agreements over the past decade, with more in the offing. What do they all add up to? Critics argue that the net results have not been very encouraging, and may indeed have detracted from WTO efforts to secure genuine multilateral agreements. Others point out that there is very little real appetite for deep integration, either through the World Trade Organisation (WTO) or within the Asian region. Few governments in Asia appear prepared to sacrifice national objectives and they only participate in regional trade agreements where they feel these objectives can be advanced. In addition old hostilities (between Japan and China for example) and new suspicions (between China and at least some ASEAN countries) are likely to put a brake on the pace of integration, at least at the East Asian level.

Probably the main reason that most countries in ASEAN, together with Japan, China and Korea, are prepared to engage in talks about closer integration is a nagging doubt that the catastrophe of 1997/98 could occur again, and that if it did, there would be little point in looking to either the United States or the Bretton Woods institutions to help them out. After 1998, the IMF lost the confidence of virtually all the major Asian economies; the widespread feeling was that it failed to grasp the serious problems in the financial systems of several Asian economies, and provided too little assistance with too many conditions after the crisis hit.[79] In spite of a decade of efforts to strengthen their economies against further external shocks, most countries in Asia realise that regimes of floating exchange rates, together with partially reformed banking systems, will not be enough to insulate them against collapses of external and internal confidence, either within ASEAN or indeed in other parts of the region, including China. Such collapses are most likely to come about as a result of political events, which in turn trigger capital flight. Optimists argue that the massive reserves of the Asian economies, together with a greater willingness to provide short-term assistance when needed, will be sufficient to prevent major capital flight and growth collapses. Others may be less confident.

Table 1: Index of GDP Growth: 1995-2006

	Malaysia	Indonesia	Thailand	Philip- pines	Vietnam
1995	100.0	100.0	100.0	100.0	100.0
1996	110.0	107.8	105.9	105.8	109.3
1997	118.1	112.9	104.4	111.3	118.3
1998	109.4	98.1	93.5	110.7	125.1
1999	116.1	98.9	97.6	114.5	131.0
2000	125.8	103.7	102.3	121.3	139.9
2001	126.8	107.6	104.6	123.4	149.6
2002	132.3	112.4	110.1	128.9	160.2
2003	139.5	117.7	117.8	135.3	171.9
2004	149.6	123.6	125.1	143.9	185.2
2005	157.3	130.7	130.6	150.9	200.9
2006	166.6	137.8	137.5	159.1	217.4

	Singapore	Korea	Taiwan	Hong Kong	China
1995	100.0	100.0	100.0	100.0	100.0
1996	107.7	106.8	106.3	104.3	109.6
1997	116.9	112.1	113.3	109.6	119.2
1998	116.7	104.6	118.5	104.2	128.5
1999	124.8	116.0	125.3	107.7	137.7
2000	137.6	126.8	132.5	118.7	148.7
2001	134.3	131.6	129.6	119.3	161.0
2002	139.9	140.9	135.6	121.4	175.6
2003	144.2	145.2	140.4	125.1	193.3
2004	157.0	152.0	149.0	135.7	212.8
2005	167.3	158.5	155.1	145.3	234.9
2006	180.5	166.6	162.3	155.5	261.0

Sources: *International Financial Statistics*, various issues between 2001 and 2008; with extra data from Bank Negara Malaysia, *Annual Report, 2006*; *Taiwan Statistical Data Book, 2007*; *Philippines Statistical Yearbook, 2007*; and Bank of Thailand web page: www.bot.or.th/bothomepage/databank/EconData.

Table 2: Per Capita Exports and Per Capita GDP, 2005 (US $)

	Exports	**GDP (1)**	**GDP (2)**
First Generation NIEs:			
Singapore	53,025	26,879	41.479
Hong Kong	41,051	26,094	35,680
South Korea	5,939	16,441	21,342
Taiwan	8,717	15,674	26,069
ASEAN-9			
Brunei	13,692	25,754	47,465
Malaysia	5,558	5,250	11,466
Thailand	1,713	2,721	6,869
Indonesia	380	1,311	3,234
Philippines	480	1,158	2,932
Vietnam	380	637	2,142
Laos	84	508	1,811
Cambodia	71	454	1,453
Myanmar	75	na	na
China	579	1,721	4,091
India	90	707	2,126

Note: GDP (1) refers to figures converted at prevailing exchange rates. GDP (2) refers to figures adjusted for differences in purchasing power parities.

Sources: Export data: *International Monetary Fund, International Financial Statistics Yearbook*, International Monetary Fund, Washington, D.C., 2007; Republic of China, *Taiwan Statistical Data Book, 2006*, Executive Yuan Council for Economic Planning and Development, Taipei, 2006. GDP data: World Bank, *International Comparison Programme: Tables of Final Results*, World Bank, Washington, D.C., 2008, Summary Table.

Table 3: Percentage Breakdown of GDP by Sector, 1995, 2000 and 2005, Thailand and Indonesia

	Thailand			Indonesia		
	1995	2000	2005	1995	2000	2005
Sector:						
Agriculture	9.5	9.0	10.2	17.4	17.2	13.4
Mining	1.2	2.4	3.1	8.8	13.9	10.4
Manufacturing	29.9	33.6	34.8	24.1	24.9	28.1
Utilities	2.4	3.0	3.1	1.2	1.3	0.9
Construction	7.2	3.1	3.1	7.6	6.1	6.4
Trade	22.2	22.8	19.5	16.6	15.7	15.8
Transport	7.2	8.0	7.4	6.8	4.9	6.6
Finance	10.5	6.3	6.5	8.7	6.4	8.4
Services	9.8	11.9	12.3	8.9	9.6	10.1
GDP	100.0	100.0	100.0	100.0	100.0	100.0
Expenditure:						
Consumption	62.3	63.2	63.7	69.0	76.6	67.3
Investment	43.5	20.8	25.3	33.4	19.0	23.6
Net exports	-5.4	14.9	10.3	-2.5	4.4	8.9
GDP	100.0	100.0	100.0	100.0	100.0	100.0

Note: Numbers do not always add to 100, because of rounding and statistical errors.

Sources: Indonesia: Bank Indonesia, *Annual Report*, various years; Thailand: Bank of Thailand web page: www.bot.or.th/bothomepage/databank/EconData.

Table 4: Welfare Indicators in Asia, c. 2000

Country	Life Expectancies		Adult	Percentage below:	
	Male	Female	Literacy	US $1	US $2
Brunei	74	79	93	na	na
Singapore	79	85	93	na	na
Malaysia	70	76	89	under 2	9
Thailand	70	75	93	under 2	33
Indonesia	68	73	88	8	52
Philippines	68	74	93	16	48
Vietnam	68	74	90	na	na
Laos	54	58	69	26	73
Cambodia	59	63	74	34	78
Myanmar	60	65	na	na	na
China	71	75	91	17	47
India	66	71	61	35	81

Sources: World Bank, *World Development Report, 2006: Equity and Development*, World Bank, Washington D.C., 2006, pp. 278-300.

Table 5: Breakdown of the Population over 15 by Educational Attainment, 2000

Educational	Thailand*	Taiwan	China	Indonesia
No education	43.5**	5.1	9.0	22.2**
Primary	20.3	18.8	32.9	38.7
Lower secondary	15.9	51.2***	39.1	17.2
Upper secondary	10.7		14.4	18.1
Tertiary	9.5	24.8	4.7	3.8

*Data for Thailand refer to the first quarter of 2001.

**Includes incompleted primary as well as those with no formal education.

***Lower and upper secondary combined.

Sources: Thailand: National Statistical Office, *Statistical Yearbook, 2001*, Office of the Prime Minister, Bangkok, 2001, p. 44; Taiwan: Republic of China, *Taiwan Statistical Data Book*, 2006, p. 26; Barry Naughton, *Chinese Economy: Transitions and Growth*, MIT Press, Cambridge, Mass., 2007, p. 196; Indonesia: Central Board of Statistics, *Population of Indonesia: Results of the 2000 Population Census, Series L2.2, Jakarta*, 2001, p. 204.

Table 6: School Participation Rates[a] in Indonesia by Expenditure Group and Location, 2003

	7-12	13-15	16-18	19-24
Urban				
Top 20%	98.9	95.4	80.0	33.5
Middle 40%	98.2	91.8	69.6	14.2
Bottom 40%	96.3	80.7	49.4	6.9
Total	97.8	89.3	66.7	19.2
Rural				
Top 20%	97.9	90.4	62.3	14.2
Middle 40%	97.2	83.6	49.6	6.0
Bottom 40%	94.8	71.0	31.1	2.7
Total	95.6	75.6	38.9	4.7

[a] Percentage of the population in the relevant age groups who are attending school.

Source: Central Board of Statistics, *Statistik Pendidikan; Survei Sosial Ekonomi Nasional* [*Education Statistics, National Socioeconomic Survey*], Jakarta, 2003.

Table 7: Governance Scores for Asian Countries: 1996 and 2005

	Voice/Government Accountability		Effectiveness		Control of Corruption	
	1996	2005	1996	2005	1996	2005
Country:						
Singapore	0.35	-0.29	2.31	2.41	2.38	2.24
Malaysia	-0.11	-0.41	0.75	1.01	0.57	0.27
Brunei	-1.04	-1.04	1.09	0.56	0.41	0.25
Thailand	-0.05	0.07	0.58	0.40	-0.33	-0.25
India	0.23	0.35	-0.45	-0.11	-0.32	-0.31
Philippines	0.11	0.01	0.22	-0.07	-0.41	-0.58
China	-1.36	-1.66	0.15	-0.11	0.00	-0.69
Vietnam	-1.39	-1.60	-0.28	-0.31	-0.68	-0.76
Indonesia	-1.22	-0.21	0.08	-0.47	-0.49	-0.86
Laos	-1.18	-1.54	-0.07	-1.09	-1.00	-1.10
Cambodia	-0.76	-0.94	-0.66	-0.94	-1.00	-1.12
Myanmar	-1.80	-2.16	-1.20	-1.61	-1.25	-1.44

Note: Countries are scored for each indicator on a scale ranging from –2.5 to +2.5. For example, on the control of corruption indicator, the worst country in 2005 (Equatorial Guinea) had a score of –1.79 and the best (Iceland) has a score of 2.49.

Source: David Kaufmann, Aart Kraay and M. Mastruzzi, *Governance Matters V: Aggregate and Individual Governance Indicators for 1996-2005*, World Bank, Washington, D.C., 2006, Appendix C.

Table 8: Exports from Asia: 1996 and 2006 (US $ billions)

Country	1996	2006	Percentage of World total 1996	2006
ASEAN				
Singapore	125.0	271.8	2.4	2.3
Malaysia	78.3	160.6	1.5	1.3
Thailand	56.0	131.0	1.1	1.1
Indonesia	49.8	103.5	1.0	0.9
Philippines	20.4	47.0	0.4	0.4
Vietnam	7.0	40.0	0.1	0.3
Other ASEAN*	3.9	13.0	...	0.1
ASEAN-10	340.4	766.9	6.6	6.4
China	151.0	969.0	2.9	8.1
Japan	411.0	650.0	7.9	5.4
South Korea	130.0	325.0	2.5	2.7
Hong Kong	181.0	317.0	3.5	2.6
Taiwan	115.7	224.0	2.2	1.9
India	33.1	120.3	0.6	1.0
Asia minus Japan	973.2	2765.3	18.8	23.0

Percentage breakdown of the increase in exports from Asia minus Japan from 1996 to 2006:

China	45.7
ASEAN-10	23.8
(Of which: Singapore	8.2)
South Korea	10.9
Hong Kong	7.6
Taiwan	6.0
(Total Old NIEs	32.7)
India	4.9
Other	1.1

*Other ASEAN: Laos, Cambodia, Brunei and Myanmar.

Source: International Monetary Fund, *International Financial Yearbook*, 2007, pp. 82-83.

Notes

1   This is a revised version of a paper originally presented at the 5th Euroseas Conference at Naples, September 2007.

2   World Bank, *The East Asian Miracle: Economic Growth and Public Policy*, World Bank, Washington, D.C. 1993.

3   The Asian Development Bank has estimated that in the five worst affected economies, the trend rate of growth since 2000 has fallen by at least 2.5 percentage points. See *Economist*, 30 June to 6 July 2007, p. 84.

4   Using the data in Table 2, the population-weighted average per capita GDP in nine ASEAN economies (excluding Myanmar) in 2005 was US $4,197 which was slightly higher than that of China. The World Bank estimates do not give any data for Myanmar, presumably because of doubts about the reliability of the official data.

5   Until the most recent Purchasing Power Parity (PPP) estimates were published in 2008, it was argued that the difference between

exchange rate and PPP conversions was especially large for China; according to Naughton this was because the prices of many non-traded goods in China such as health and housing were low compared with other parts of Asia (Barry Naughton, *The Chinese Economy: Transitions and Growth*, MIT Press, Cambridge, Mass. 2007, p. 226). But it would appear that, as government provision was cut back after 1990, costs of housing and other services in China are rapidly catching up with countries such as the Philippines, Thailand and Indonesia. Thus the PPP-adjusted data used by the World Bank may no longer reflect reality.

6 Prema-Chandra Athukorala, 'Post-Crisis Export Performance: The Indonesian Experience in Regional Perspective', *Bulletin of Indonesian Economic Studies*, Vol. 42 (2), 2006, Table 3.

7 David Green, 'Bridging the ASEAN Development Divide: A Regional Overview', *ASEAN Economic Bulletin*, Vol. 24 (1), 2007, p. 19.

8 It has been claimed that in both Indonesia and Thailand, infrastructure is worse than a decade ago and this has affected investment by both foreign and domestic businesses (*Economist*, 30 June to 6 July 2007, p. 84).

9 Chris Manning and Kurnya Roesad, 'Survey of Recent Developments', *Bulletin of Indonesian Economic Studies*, Vol. 42 (2), August 2006, Table 4.

10 Central Board of Statistics, *Statistik Indonesia, 2005/6* [*Statistical Yearbook of Indonesia, 2005*], Central Board of Statistics, Jakarta, 2006, pp. 66-71.

11 National Statistical Office, *Statistical Year Book 2001*, National Statistical Office, Office of the Prime Minister, Bangkok, 2001, p. 37. For an analysis of the impact of minimum wages in the urban formal sector in Indonesia, see Asep W. Suryahadi, D. Perwira and Sudarno Sumarto, 'Minimum Wage Policy and its Impact on Employment in

the Urban Formal Sector', *Bulletin of Indonesian Economic Studies*, Vol. 39 (1), April, 2003, pp. 29-50. For a general overview of the legislation affecting employment and minimum wages in the post-Soeharto era see Chris Manning and Kurnya Roesad, 'The Manpower Law of 2003 and its Implementing Regulations: Genesis, Key Articles and Potential Impact', *Bulletin of Indonesian Economic Studies*, Vol. 43 (1), April, 2007, pp. 59-86. Warr examines the impact of minimum wage legislation on poverty in Thailand (Peter Warr, 'Globalization, Growth and Poverty Reduction in Thailand', *ASEAN Economic Bulletin*, Vol. 21 (1), 2004, pp 1-18.

12 Some of the assertions which have appeared in the literature regarding increases in poverty and unemployment in Thailand and Indonesia as a result of the crisis are greatly exaggerated. For example Stiglitz claimed that poverty doubled. It is not clear whether he means numbers of poor, or the headcount measure of poverty, but neither in fact doubled. He also claimed that the unemployment rate increased threefold in Thailand and tenfold in Indonesia, which again is a gross exaggeration (Joseph Stiglitz, *Globalization and its Discontents*, Penguin Books, London, 2002, p. 97).

13 Medhi Krongkaew and Nanak Kakwani, 'The growth-equity trade-off in modern economic development: the case of Thailand', *Journal of Asian Economics*, Vol. 14, 2003, Table 5.

14 Warr, *loc. cit.*, Table 2.

15 Central Board of Statistics, *op. cit.*, p. 565.

16 There was an increase in the headcount measure of poverty and the numbers below the poverty line (to 17.8 million between February 2005 and March 2006). This was attributed to the sharp increase in the domestic price of rice (M. Chatib Basri and A. A. Patunru, 'Survey of Recent Developments', *Bulletin of Indonesian Economic Studies*, Vol. 42 (3), 2006, pp. 308-9).

17 More recent evidence indicates that in 2006, 7.4 per cent of the Indonesian population fell below the dollar a day standard, compared with 10.3 per cent in China in 2004. The conclusion is that Indonesia's growth has been more pro-poor than in China (Bert Hofman, Min Zhao and Y. Ishihara, 'Asian Development Strategies: China and Indonesia Compared', *Bulletin of Indonesian Economic Studies*, Vol. 43 (2), 2007, p. 174). To what extent the recent revisions in PPP estimates of income and consumption in China and other Asian countries will change the picture given in Table 4 is still unclear.

18 According to Balisacan, the headcount measure of poverty in the Philippines declined from 41 per cent in 1985 to 25 per cent in 1997; there was an increase to 27.5 per cent in 2000 (Arsenio Balisacan, 'Poverty and inequality', in Arsenio Balisacan and Hal Hill (eds), *The Philippines Economy: Development Policies and Challenges*, Oxford University Press, Oxford, 2003, p. 319.

19 World Bank, *World Development Report 2006: Equity and Development*, World Bank, Washington, D.C. 2006, p. 279.

20 See, for example, *Financial Times*, 5 December 1996.

21 Ammar Siamwalla has argued that the Bank of Thailand's handling of the problems in the Bangkok Bank of Commerce (BBC) was an important factor leading to its loss of reputation. The excessive leniency showed to the BBC was in part the result of the fact that the BBC had made loans to the Governor of the Bank of Thailand. This fact emerged in a no-confidence debate in the Thai parliament (Ammar Siamwalla, *Picking up the Pieces: Bank and Corporate Restructuring in post-1997 Thailand*, TDRI, Bangkok, 2001, p. 19).

22 Akira Suehiro, 'Who manages and who damages the Thai economy? The technocracy, the four core agencies and Dr Puey's networks', in S. Takashi and P. Abinales (eds), *After the Crisis:*

Hegemony, Technocracy and Governance in Southeast Asia, Kyoto University Press, 2005, p. 42.

23 Joseph Stiglitz, *op. cit.*, p. 99.

24 According to Akira Suehiro, financial liberalisation was promoted by the Bank of Thailand, but was also beneficial to the economic interests of many *Chart Thai* MPs (Akira Suehiro, *loc. cit.*, 2005, p. 39). External pressure from the IMF and the World Bank might also have been important but it is unlikely that this would have been sufficient to bring about policy changes without the support of powerful domestic groups. Neither the World Bank nor the IMF had much leverage over Thai policies in the early 1990s, although the Thai government was sensitive to the effect that criticism might have on its international reputation.

25 The Bank of Thailand did try to introduce Chile-type measures, including a compulsory deposit requirement for capital inflows. According to Ammar Siamwalla these had little effect (Ammar Siamwalla, *op. cit.*, p. 18). The Bank of Thailand also wanted the government to run a much tighter fiscal policy in 1994 to cool the economy down but the government in fact ran a budget deficit. This would seem to support the argument made by Suehiro that the 'four agency' system established in the 1960s had largely broken down by the early 1990s, and there was little coordination of fiscal and monetary policy.

26 Boediono, 'Problems of Implementing Monetary Policy', in Ross Macleod (ed.), *Indonesia Assessment 1994: Finance as a Key Sector in Indonesia's Development*, ISEAS, Singapore, 1994, pp. 121-22.

27 David C. Cole and Betty Slate, *Building a Modern Financial System: The Indonesian Experience*, Cambridge University Press, Cambridge, 1996, p. 356.

28 John Chant and Mari Pangestu, 'An Assessment of Financial Reform in Indonesia, 1983-1999', in Gerard Caprio, Izak Atiyas and

James A. Hansen (eds), *Financial Reform: Theory and Experience*, Cambridge University Press, Cambridge, 1996, pp. 254-55.

29 Boediono, *loc. cit.*, p. 124.

30 Z. A. Yusof *et al.*, 'Financial Reform in Malaysia', in Caprio, Atiyas, and Hansen (eds), *op. cit.*, pp. 290-96.

31 Natalia Tamarisa, 'Do the Macroeconomic Effects of Capital Controls Vary by Type', *ASEAN Economic Bulletin*, Vol. 23 (2), 2006, p. 137; K. S. Jomo, 'Were Malaysia's Capital Controls Effective?', in K. S. Jomo, (ed.), *After the Storm: Crisis, Recovery and Sustaining Development in Four Asian Economies*, Singapore University Press, Singapore, 2004, p. 192; Prema-Chandra Athukorala, 'Capital Account Regimes, Crisis and Adjustment in Malaysia', *Asian Development Review*, Vol. 18 (1), 2000, p. 20.

32 Prema-Chandra Athukorala and Peter G. Warr, 'Vulnerability to a Currency Crisis: Lessons from the Asian Experience', *World Economy*, Vol. 25 (1), 2002, Tables 1, 2 and 3.

33 Jonathan Pincus and Rizal Ramli, 'Deepening or Hollowing Out: Financial Liberalization, Accumulation and Indonesia's Economic Crisis', in Jomo (ed.), *op. cit.*, Table 5.5.

34 Helmut Reisen, 'Domestic Causes of Currency Crisis: Policy Lessons for Crisis Avoidance', *OECD Development Centre, Technical Papers No. 136*, June 1998, Table 4.

35 Anne Booth, 'The Causes of South East Asia's Economic Crisis: A Sceptical Review of the Debate', *Asia Pacific Business Review*, Vol. 8 (2), 2001, pp. 22-23.

36 Natasha Hamilton-Hart, 'Indonesia: Reforming the Institutions of Financial Governance?', in Greg Noble and John Ravenhill (eds), *The Asian Financial Crisis and the Architecture of Global Finance*, Cambridge University Press, Cambridge, 2000, p. 111.

37 Several authors have contrasted the volatility in economies such as Thailand and Indonesia with the apparently greater stability

in Vietnam and China, which had, and still have, capital controls. Even the World Bank conceded that China and Vietnam were 'sheltered from the crisis due in part to their lesser reliance on short-term foreign borrowing and portfolio flows' (World Bank, *East Asia: Recovery and Beyond*, World Bank, Washington, D.C., 2000, p. 68). China did, however, experience a growth slowdown in the latter part of the 1990s (Hongying Wang, 'Dangers and Opportunities: The Implications of the Asian Financial Crisis for China', in Greg Noble and John Ravenhill (eds), *The Asian Financial Crisis and the Architecture of Global Finance*, Cambridge University Press, Cambridge, 2000, pp. 152-55). More recently it has been argued that the capital controls in China are not working, and a 'de facto openness' now characterises the capital account in China (Naughton, *op. cit.*, pp. 421-22).

38　For detailed case studies of the borrowing strategies of three large Indonesian conglomerates, see Yasuyuki Matsumoto, *Financial Fragility and Instability in Indonesia*, Routledge, Abingdon, 2007, Chapters 6, 8 and 9.

39　For a good discussion of the demanding conditions under which a currency board could function, see Barry Eichengreen, 'The International Monetary Fund in the Wake of the Asian Crisis', in Noble and Ravenhill (eds), *op. cit.*, pp. 173-5. The policy climate in Indonesia in early 1998 was such that none of these conditions could have been met.

40　Yuri Sato, 'Bank restructuring and financial institution reform in Indonesia', *Developing Economies*, Vol. 43 (1), 2005, p. 103.

41　*Ibid.*, Table 1.

42　*Ibid.*, p. 93; see also Olivier Frecaut, 'Indonesia's Banking Crisis: A New Perspective on US $50 Billion of Losses', *Bulletin of Indonesian Economic Studies*, Vol. 40 (1), 2004, p. 41.

43 In 2001, interest payments on domestic debt, much of it bank restructuring bonds, amounted to six per cent of GDP. Total development expenditures were only three per cent of GDP (Reza Siregar, 'Survey of Recent Developments', *Bulletin of Indonesian Economic Studies*, Vol. 37 (3), 2001, Table 2).

44 In addition it has been argued that monetary policy in Thailand after 2000 was too tight. Nidhiprabha argues that, in addition to the tight monetary and fiscal policies imposed on Thailand by IMF conditions in 1997/98, the monetary authorities made a further error in June 2001 in raising interest rates at a time when monetary policy should have been eased (B. Nidhiprabha, 'Thailand's Macroeconomic Policy after July 1997', *Asian Economic Papers*, Vol. 2 (1), 2003, pp. 158-71). Once again this probably reflected poor communication between different agencies in the Thai government.

45 Ammar Siamwalla, *op. cit.*, p. 34.

46 But some conglomerates did try to get control of their banks back from IBRA; for a discussion of the Bank Lippo story see Daniel Fitzpatrick, 'Tinkering around the Edges: Inadequacy of Corporate Governance Reform in Post-Crisis Indonesia', in M. Chatib Basri and Pierre van der Eng, (eds) *Business in Indonesia: New Challenges, Old Problems*, ISEAS, Singapore, 2004, pp. 182-3. After the crisis IBRA had a large stake in the bank; there were allegations that the Riady family tried to drive down the share price in order to buy back a controlling interest in the bank at a devalued price.

47 Pincus and Ramli, *loc. cit.*, p. 128.

48 World Bank, *op. cit.*, 2000, p. 68.

49 International Monetary Fund, *The IMF and Recent Capital Account Crisis: Indonesia, Korea, Brazil*, IMF, Independent Evaluation Office, Washington, 2003, pp. 71-72; The three banks were owned

by the Salim group, the Danamon group and the Gajah Tunggal groups respectively. Together with one state bank (EXIM Bank), these banks received around 75 per cent of all the liquidity credits granted by the central bank (*ibid.*, p. 72). Details of the Gajah Tunggal's group's offshore syndicated borrowings through BDNI are given in Matsumoto, *op. cit.*, Table 9.5. In 1996, the Nursalim family, who controlled the Gadjah Tunggal conglomerate, sold their shares in BDNI to an affiliated company, a sale which brought them over US $300 million.

50 The Sinar Mas story has attracted several analyses; see Matsumoto, *op. cit.* Chapter 8; Romain Pirard and Rofikoh Rokhim, 'Asia Pulp and Paper Indonesia: The Business Rationale that Led to Forect Degradation and Financial Collapse', Working Paper 31, Center for International Forestry Research, CIFOR, Bogor, 2005; and Rajeswary A. Brown, 'Conglomerates in Contemporary Indonesia', *Southeast Asia Research*, Vol. 12 (6), 2004, pp. 392-401.

51 See the quotation from Larry Lang in Akira Suehiro, 'Family Business Gone Wrong? Ownership Patterns and Corporate Performance in Thailand', ADB Institute Working Paper, 19, ADB Institute, Tokyo, 2001, p. 22.

52 Sato examined the post-crisis changes which occurred in Indonesia between 1996 and 2000. She also found that firms with tight family control did not perform worse than those with more dispersed ownership (Yuri Sato, 'Corporate Ownership and Management in Indonesia: Does it Change?', in Basri and van der Eng (eds), *op. cit.*, pp. 21-58. Suehiro analysed the performance of a number of Thai listed companies after the crisis, and found that family-owned companies were not always poor performers; corporations where ownership was dispersed tended to be the worst performers Suehiro, *op. cit.*, 2001).

53 Bambang Brodjonegoro, 'The Effects of Decentralisation on Business in Indonesia', in M. Chatib Basri and Pierre van der Eng, *Business in Indonesia: New Challenges, Old Problems*, ISEAS, Singapore, 2004, p. 139.

54 The Indonesian and Malaysian currencies were never pegged to the dollar, and did in fact decline against the dollar between 1990 and 1997. Williamson has argued that the crawling peg system adopted by the Indonesian authorities worked quite well after 1986, and the decision in late August 1997 to abandon it and allow the rupiah to float freely was a crucial mistake which precipitated the problems in the last four months of 1997 (John Williamson, 'The Years of Emerging Market Crises: A Review of Feldstein', *Journal of Economic Literature*, 2004, Vol. (1), pp. 822-37.

55 Some observers have argued that, as a result of the crisis, governments in Asia have kept their currencies low against the dollar to promote exports, a strategy which has led to a rapid accumulation of foreign exchange reserves. But this seems true only of China, and to some extent Malaysia, at least until 2005.

56 International Monetary Fund, *op. cit.*, p. 64.

57 Anne Booth, 'Linking, De-Linking and Re-linking: Southeast Asia in the Global Economy in the Twentieth Century', *Australian Economic History Review*, Vol. 44 (1), 2004, p. 38.

58 Francis Ng and Alexander Yeats, 'Major Trade Trends in East Asia: What are their Implications for Regional Cooperation and Growth?', Policy Research Working Paper, 3084, World Bank, Washington, 2003, p. 3.

59 *Ibid.*, Tables 1.1 and 5.1.

60 An important point to emerge from Table 8 is that the 'old NIES', or the original four tigers accounted for more than one third of the increase in exports from Asia minus Japan between 1996 and

2006. They remain formidable export-producing economies, both to other parts of Asia and to the wider world.

61 Ng and Yeats, *loc. cit.*, Table 5.1.

62 Siow-Yue Chia, 'ASEAN-China Economic Competition and Free Trade Area', *Asian Economic Papers*, Vol. 4 (1), 2005, p. 116.

63 *Ibid.*, Table 5.

64 Green, *loc. cit.*, p. 31.

65 Chia, *loc. cit.*, Table 3.

66 David R. Holst and John Weiss, 'ASEAN and China: Export Rivals or Partners in Regional Growth?', *World Economy*, Vol. 27 (8), 2004, p. 1263.

67 Ng and Yeats, *loc. cit.*, p. 63.

68 Sanjaya Lall, 'Foreign Direct Investment, Technology Development, and Competitiveness: Issues and Evidence', in S. Lall and S. Urata (eds), *Competitiveness, Foreign Direct Investment and Technological Activity in East Asia*, Edward Elgar, Cheltenham, 2003, p. 30.

69 Athukorala, *loc. cit.*, 2006, pp. 206-7.

70 *Ibid.*, pp. 206-7

71 Baldwin has argued that less than three per cent of intra-ASEAN trade in 1999 benefited from AFTA's preferences. He suggested that most firms found the bureaucratic procedures required to gain preferential access too cumbersome, especially as there was often very little difference between the MFN and the preferential tariff anyway (Richard Baldwin, 'Managing the Noodle Bowl: The Fragility of East Asian Regionalism', CEPR Discussion Paper 5561, March 2006, p. 10).

72 Chia, *loc. cit.*, p. 137.

73 Baldwin, *loc. cit.*, p. 14.

74 Chia, *loc. cit.*, pp. 141-44.

75 According to estimates of Gill and Kharas, 49 per cent of East Asia's trade was within the region in 2000-4, which is only

slightly lower than the percentage for the EU (Indermit Gill and Homi Kharas, *An East Asian Renaissance: Ideas for Economic Growth*, World Bank, Washington, D.C. 2006, p. 6). We should bear in mind that it has been suggested that an Exchange Rate Mechanism (ERM)-type mechanism may work in the Asian context. See Peter Wilson, 'Prospects for Asian Exchange Rate Co-operation: Why an ERM Solution Might be the Most Palatable', *Journal of the Asia Pacific Economy*, Vol. 11 (1), 2006, pp. 1-34.

76 Barry Eichengreen, 'What to do with the Chiangmai Initiative', *Asian Economic Papers*, Vol. 2 (1), 2003, pp. 8-11.

77 *Economist*, 30 June to 6 July 2007, p. 84.

78 Gill and Kharas, *op. cit.*, p. 29.

79 See Chris Giles, 'Wrong Lessons from Asia's Crisis', *Financial Times*, 2 July 2007.

www.ingramcontent.com/pod-product-compliance
Lightning Source LLC
Chambersburg PA
CBHW022130280326
41933CB00007B/629